A BEGINNER'S GUIDE to BECOMING an ANTIQUES DEALER

C A PYM

© Whilst every care has been taken in the compilation of this Guide, the author accepts no liability for any financial or other loss incurred by reliance placed on the information, general views, opinions or suggestions contained within it.
2012 by the author of this book.

The book author retains sole copyright to his or her contributions to this book. All Rights Reserved. No part of this publication may be reproduced, stored in a retrieval system, or transmitted in any form or by any means, electronic, mechanical, photocopying, recording or otherwise, without the prior written permission of the copyright owner.

blurb

FORWARD

For the last 30 years, I have worked my way, with a hands-on approach, from collecting and studying antiques and collectibles as a hobby all the way through to running a successful professional business. It seems appropriate to depart some of that knowledge of a very popular and fascinating profession to an ever increasing inquisitive public.

DEDICATION

I wish to dedicate this book to the memory of my late dear father who was an upstanding local citizen and left his mark despite battling a long debilitating illness.

ACKNOWLEDGEMENTS

All photographs supplied courtesy of David J Pym Antiques, (www.davidjpym.com).

Front Cover imagery and artistic effects by Christopher Sadler and Abigail Pym, Photographic, Fashion and Textile Undergraduate Students

RENE LALIQUE - 'SUZANNE' - c1925

CONTENTS	**Page**
1. Introduction:	1-2
Historic Periods	3-16
2. Starting Points	18-20
3. Specialist Areas	21-24
4. Reproductions and Fakes	26-29
5. Buy Antiques	30-36
6. Restoration	37-42
7. Retailing	43-45
8. Statutory Rules and Criteria	46-47
9. Online Auction Websites	49-52
10. Fine Antiques	54-57
Features:	
Militaria (Dueling Pistols)	55-57
Rene Lalique	58-61
Moorcroft Pottery	63-66
WMF	68-69
Jewellery	70-75
11. Conclusion	76
12. Top Ten Tips	77

INTRODUCTION

The world of Antiques is both fascinating and inexhaustible.... England has a rich and colorful history which is probably one of the most envied in the World and this heritage has afforded us a varied tapestry of antiques and collectibles. This includes pottery, pewter and silver in the 16th and 17th centuries, early beautiful porcelain from 1750 in Europe, coveted early Georgian furniture through to a hugely productive 19th century Victorian period with fine antiques, and collectibles of both a decorative, emotive and amusement nature.

The term 'antique' loosely describes items and artifacts made one hundred or more years ago. This had been due to earlier tax laws, although within the trade today, the term also broadly encompasses the period prior to the end of World War II. Very few items were actually made during the war because many factories were requisitioned for the war effort, thereby ceasing production. Some prime factories such as Meissen and Dresden in Germany, suffered significant damage or socioeconomic depression. All of this, therefore, created a void at the end of the Art Deco period until the industry found its feet. Eventually the Retro period, mainly influenced by America, took effect in the 1950's and 1960's.

HISTORIC PERIODS

1. **GEORGIAN AND RECENCY** are periods of history normally defined as spanning the reigns of the first four Hanoverian kings of Great Britain (later the United Kingdom): George I, George II, George III and George IV. The era covers the period from 1714 to 1830, incorporating the sub-period of the Regency defined by the regency of George IV as Prince of Wales during the illness of his father George III.

The term 'Georgian' is typically used in the contexts of social history, architecture and antiques. The Regency Period is also used in antique terms.

Georgian society and its preoccupations were well portrayed in the novels of writers such as Henry Fielding, Mary Shelley and Jane Austen, characterised by the architecture of Robert Adam, John Nash and James Wyatt and the emergence of the Gothic Revival style, which hearkened back to a supposed golden age emergence of the Romantic poets, principally through Samuel Taylor Coleridge, William Wordsworth, Percy Bysshe Shelley, William Blake, John Keats, Lord Byron and Robert Burns. Their work ushered in a new era of poetry, characterised by vivid and colourful language, evocative of elevating idea and themes.

The paintings of Thomas Gainsborough, Sir Joshua Rynolds and the young J.M.W. Turner and John Constable illustrated the changing world of the Georgian period - as did the work of designers like Capability Brown, the landscape designer.

It was a time of immense social change in Britain, with the beginnings of the Industrial Revolution which began the process of intensifying class divisions, and the emergence of rival political parties like the Whigs and Tories.

In terms of antiques, it has left a wealth of stylised, romantic antiques such as silver, porcelain, furniture and works of art, which today are highly regarded and can command large sums of money.

However, many such antiques and works of art are preserved family heirlooms housed within surviving stately homes and country estates and therefore, infrequently reach the open market. The length of time has also contributed to the scarcity and rarity of such items surviving in good condition.

Regency Clocks, dueling pistols, militaria and jewellery are examples of fine workmanship and, hence, have become highly prized rare collectibles.

2. THE VICTORIAN ERA of British history was the period of Queen Victoria's reign from 20 June 1837 until her death on 22 January 1901. Culturally, there was a transition away from the rationalism of Georgian period and towards romanticism and mysticism with regard to religion, social values, and the arts.

In 1851 the Great Exhibition, the first World Fair showcased the latest innovations. At its centre was Crystal Palace, a modular glass and iron structure.

Victorian decorative arts refers to the style of decorative arts during the Victorian era. Victorian design is widely viewed as having indulged in grand excess of ornament and the era is known for its interpretation and eclectic revival of historic styles mixed with the introduction of middle east and Asian influences in furniture, fittings and Interior decoration. The Arts and Crafts movement , the aesthetic movement, Anglo-Japanese style, and Art Nouveau have their beginnings in the late Victorian era.

Wallpaper was often made in elaborate floral patterns with primary colors in the backgrounds (red, blue and yellow), and o overprinted with colors of cream and tan. This was followed by Gothic art inspired papers in earth tones with stylized leaf and floral patterns. William Morris was one of the most influential designers of wallpaper and fabrics during the latter half of the Victorian period. Morris was inspired and used Medieval and Gothic tapestries in his work.

From the 1850's interiors became very borgious with heavy curtains displaying privacy and funeral customs were marked by photographic records. Queen Victoria's own private mourning of Prince Albert reflected the somber mood by black stoneware and porcelain and dark jewellery.

Natural history became increasingly an "amateur's" activity. Particularly in Britain and the United States this grew into

LORENZYL COLD PAINTED BRONZE c1930

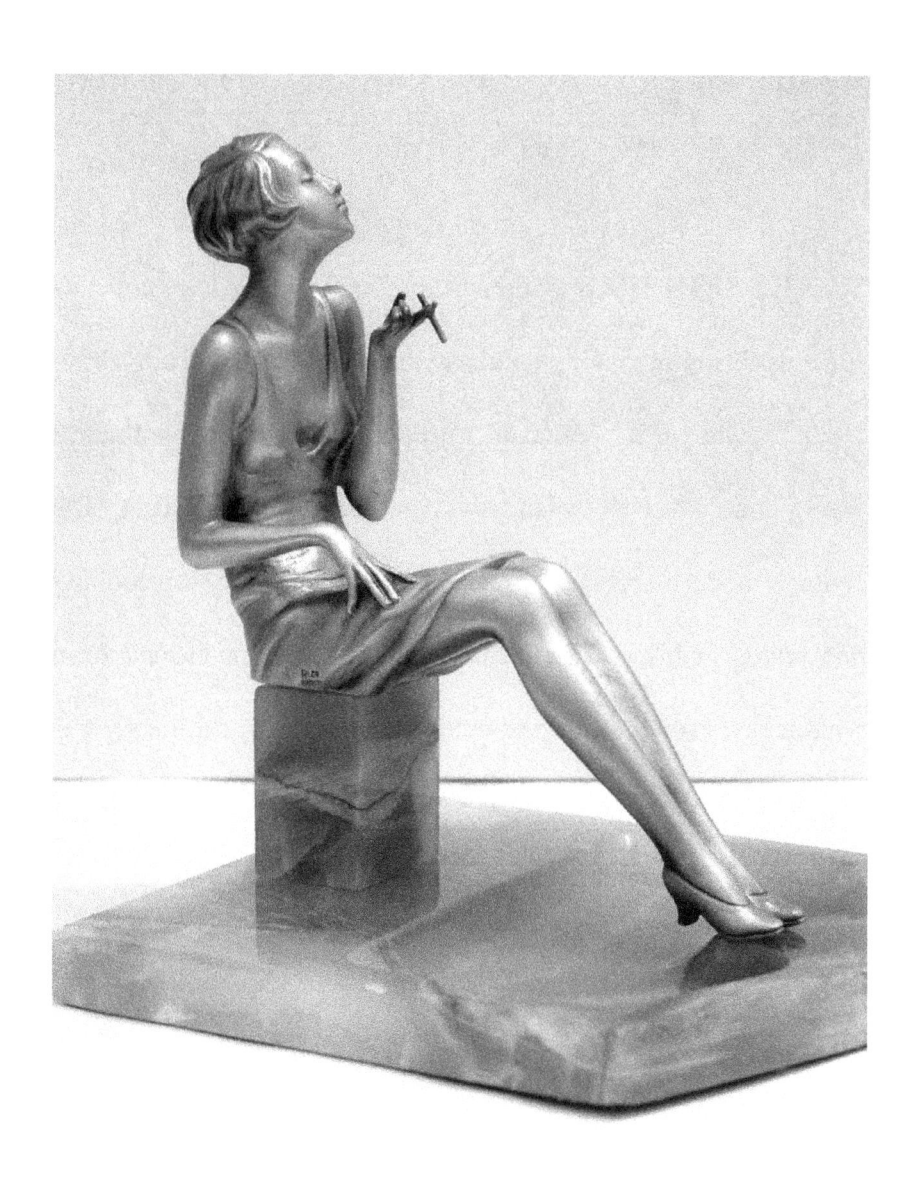

hobbies such as the study of birds, butterflies, seashells, beetles and wild flowers, all of which are recorded influences in art designs on porcelain and pottery.

3. ART NOUVEAU is French for "new art". Also known as Jugendstil, German for "youth style" and is dated from 1890-1910. It was most popular in Europe but its eventual influence was global. Art Nouveau could be said to be the first 20th century modern style and it was the first style to stop looking backwards in history for ideas, taking inspiration instead from what it saw around it, in particular, the natural world. Its style is depicted:

* sinuous, elongated curvy lines
* the whiplash line
* vertical lines and height
* stylized flowers, leaves, roots, buds and seedpods
* the female form - in a pre-Raphaelite pose with long,

flowing hair

* exotic woods, marquetry, iridescent glass, silver and semi-precious stones.

Influences:

* arts and crafts - art nouveau shared the same belief in good quality and fine craftsmanship but was happy with mass production

* rococo style

* botanical research

Important Names:

* Charles René MacKintosh -

- architect and designer of furniture and jewellery

* Alphonse Mucha - posters

* Aubrey Beardsley - book illustrations

* Louis Comfort Tiffany - lighting

* René Lalique - glass and jewellery

* Emile Galle - ceramics, glass and furniture

GOLDSCHEIDER WALL MASK c1930

* Victor Horta - architect

* WMF - stylised 'lady figure' and arts and craft- silver-plated pewter tableware

* Moorcroft - pottery

This was a highly influential and stylised period which has become one of the most iconic and highly collected.

Due to mass production, many art nouveau pieces are not valuable although still highly desirable. However, if the item is made by a famous and accredited designer, theprice soars (see later section Fine Antiques).

4. ART DECO (c1908 to 1935) began in Europe, particularly Paris. in the early years of the 20th century. It didn't really take hold until after World War I and it reigned until the outbreak of World War II. This time the style was depicted by:

* geometric and angular shap

* chrome, glass, shiny fabrics, mirrors and mirror tiles

* Stylized images of airplanes, cars, cruise liners and skyscrapers

* nature motifs - shells, sunrises, flowers and furs.

Influences:

* art nouveau - kept the nature motifs of its predecessor But discarded its flowing organic shape and pastels for bolder materials and colours such as chrome and black.

* cubism - painters such as Picasso were experimenting with space, angles and geometry:

* Early Hollywood -the glamorous world of the silver screen filtered through to design using shiny fabrics subdued lighting, and mirrors.

* Cocktail cabinet and smoking paraphernalia became highly fashionable.

Some Names: Eileen Gray - furniture

Raymond Templier - jewellery

Clarice Cliff - china
René Lalique - glass and jewellery

Moorcroft - pottery

Other influences:

* 1912 RMS Titanic sank

* 1922 Tutankhamen's tomb discovered

* 1922 Ulysses by James Joyce published

* 1931 Empire State Building completed

Film stars:

> Greta Garbo
>
> Marlene Dietrich
>
> Fred Astaire
>
> Ginger Rogers

* The charleston and tango were the latest dance crazes, jazz was born and singer Josephine Baker thrilled Paris.

5. RETRO - A culturally outdated or aged style, trend, mode or fashion from the overall post-modern past, that has since that time become functionally or superficially norm once again. The use of "retro" style iconography and imagery interjected into post-modern art, advertising, mass media etc. It generally implies a vintage of at least 15 or 20 years.

In terms of the Antiques Trade, the 1940's and 1950's, in particular, began mainly in the United States with such rock artistes as Buddy Holly and Elvis Presley being predominantly influential in the music world and fashion. So too leather handbags, "bell-bottom jeans", big sunglasses, fedoras, funk jackets (commonly called Adidas Classics) and shoes, small neckties, chiffon scarves, sports equipment, skinny jeans etc. Makeup may also play a part in feminine retro fashions, with focal points being heavily-lined eyes and bright red lipstick; hairstyles such as pompadours, ponytails and ducktails may be adopted as well as styles that model film stars of the 1940's and 1950's.

This continued into the 1960's and 1970's in particular in Britain with such rock influences as Led Zeppelin, Black Sabbath, Jimi Hendrix, The Beatles and Pink Floyd. Fashion too became iconic with psychedelic genre shapes, and bold colours with such designers as Mary Quant.

Later in the 1970's Biba and Laura Ashley became iconic high street names providing retro and vintage fashion. They are still in existence today.

RARE WMF DESK INK STAND c1920

STARTING POINTS

One well known successful dealer when asked to describe the secret of success stated:

"to have for sale a pot of gold at a next to nothing price"

In other words, as close as possible to a quality or valuable item at the cheapest possible price.

The most important feature of an antique or collector's item is its uniqueness, the fact the item was made at a time when labour and man hours were at a premium and nine times out of ten, those skills could not be replicated today for the same price. The fact too, that the item cannot be found in the High Street Shops makes it immediately more desirable.

One of the most important attributes of being a dealer is an 'eye' or a keen awareness of artistic taste, fine detail and value. A person is most likely born with an artistic eye; however, having a keen interest, such as a collector's hobby in a specialist area, coupled with knowledge gained from a plethora of reference books on the chosen subject, is the most frequent entry point. Marketing and industry knowledge can be gained through experience and a hands-on approach of trial and error.

The dealer may also have special areas of knowledge or expertise that he already used in a previous employment - for example, engineering, electronics, horology, carpentry or specific restoration skills. Any of these could be used on their own to develop a specific area of expertise or hobby to supplement and assist an established dealer or retailer.

Other requisites such as marketing, presentation and sales to 'front' a retail business will have been learnt through employment and general life skills. Once again, the extent to which a person would wish to be involved may be decided initially perhaps as a hobby or interest supplementary to a full time employment.

One of the most appealing characteristics of the Antiques business is the scope and endless variances each item will offer together with its own unique history and the fact that different and, hitherto unknown, items are constantly being discovered. There are no precise benchmark. The value of an item is dictated by the current market. This makes the antiques business particularly exciting but on the other hand, there is a long learning curve which to all extent is indefinite. Also, the business is transitory i.e. it is subject to fashions, trends and economic fluctuations.

SPECIALIST AREAS

One of best ways to decide your specialist area, if you have not already done so, is to visit Auction Rooms to see the types of items for sale in the raw, or Antique Fairs where particular collections are showcased by individual dealers, or Antique Arcades which encompass a wide range of different articles of every description. Ultimately, shops or specialist Retail Units will show items in their best, possibly restored, and expertly presented, condition.

It will most likely be an area in which you have a particular interest or one you feel most comfortable with. It is important to remember, however, that most dealer's collections will have been obtained over a long period of time and will have required careful and painstaking selection and research. That is not to say, of course, that a great deal of pleasure will have been experienced in searching for them and owning them and it is safe to say that the charm of antiques/collectibles is that it would be impossible for any one person or persons, no matter how experienced or knowledgeable, to ever be considered an 'absolute' expert. There is always something new to learn.

The antiques world is constantly changing worldwide and is governed by fashions and economic climate. Although, as a general rule of thumb, an item which at is inception was an item of quality and skilled manufacture and/or intrinsic artistic value, will predominantly retain that mark of quality and desirability throughout its existence which, in turn, will be reflected in its open market price.

However, new discoveries are made all the time, where an item has lain in a private collection and its like not seen before, or its worth or desirability is undervalued by an owner who may have inherited it, and it subsequently comes up for sale possibly at a boot fair or house clearance auction. Over the passage of time many different styles of all types of artifact have been made and it would be impossible to ever perceive to attempt to account for every single item.

Many times has it been said *'if only I had kept so-and-so item. Look how much it is worth now'*. But that is precisely the nature of antiques that no-one could possibly predict for sure what would be a valuable item or collectible in the future. Not even René Lalique or William Moorcroft knew how desirable their products would be during their lifetimes. However, a savvy dealer or collector may use his knowledge and expertise and choose those articles which **he** considers could potentially have the 'x factor' and thereby make himself a pot of gold. A buyer too might purchase an undervalued item simply because he likes it and wants to enjoy it in his home or otherwise, it is a utilitarian artifact which has been particularly well made or is unique and better quality than anything similar of modern manufacture.

Other articles are already accredited, or are items to look out for (see Fine Antiques Section). Such is the mystery and excitement of antiques.

Condition is all important and although 'old stapled repairs' on pieces of porcelain and china denote character, the most desired condition to command the best price will be as near perfect to its new state as possible.

RENE LALIQUE 'CEYLAN' opal/blue c1924

REPRODUCTIONS AND FAKES

It is important to note at this stage, an item whose condition is 'too perfect' will immediately arouse suspicion as to whether it is a reproduction or fake and it is only through knowledge and research that a dealer would be able to test its authenticity. As a general rule of thumb, if the seller is unsure of an item's originality and age, the best advice is not to make any assertions or assumptions as that could be construed as misleading statements or, in the worse case scenario, a trade description misrepresentation that could even result in legal action.

Throughout history, very clever, painstaking, reproductions have been made. For example, some 19th century pieces of furniture are actually reproductions of styles 100 years earlier, or pieces may have been changed or modified, all of which will have a bearing on the price. This is why antiques are exhaustive and fascinating but ultimately they can, in the case of 'Fine Antiques' i.e. those which have a proven track record or pedigree, be a substantive investment. The arts and antiques investment market is considered to be of a more speculative nature, however; large sums of money can be realised even over short periods of time, if the investment is wise and considered.

That is why it is extremely important that any item for resale should be thoroughly researched in order that correct information may be offered to a prospective buyer. This is a unique criteria of the Antiques Industry as other retail establishments will source their products directly from factories or warehouses in the full knowledge of the precise origins of their merchandise having been manufactured yesterday. One of the most compelling qualities of antiques or collectibles is that they are items which are unlikely to be found in the High Street Shops and it is that quality which must be qualified and clarified as there is nothing more infuriating to a purchaser than to later discover that his treasured 'antique' is in fact a modern fake.

There are, however, many trading opportunities for all manner of variations of age, condition and style as already explained, provided the item is correctly described.

It is considered good practice within the industry, to obtain a full detailed written receipt on headed paper at the point of purchase. This is certainly the case for 'fine antiques'. This will authenticate the sale, provide details for future contact and insurance purposes. From the dealer's prospective, he will also need to retain copies of all purchases and sales in order to correlate his books for tax purposes (for discussion in a later section).

An antique business proprietor, in common will all other retail establishments and businesses, will prove the success and longevity of his business if he operates in a professional, and trustworthy manner. This will help to build longterm relationships.

BUY ANTIQUES

AUCTION ROOMS: are constantly an area of mystery and intrigue. They are not new, many dating back several hundreds of years and they are an excellent means of selling and buying unwanted and/or valuable items.

Their apparent mystery lies in the inherent 'risk' of making any gesture which might be construed as a 'bid' at an inopportune and unintentional point in the proceedings of the Auction. Once a bid has been made', the law requires the bidder to pay for the item, together with the published charges of the Auction Room.

This is not as precarious as it may seem because a bidder is registered before the start of the Auction, and his/her allocated bid number (paddle) is required to validate any purchase of any lot during the sale. The most 'risk' would be in the case where a bidder becomes 'carried away' within the Auction process and ends up paying well in excess of his intended budget or alternatively, he fails to note that there is as much as 25 per cent charges added on top of the hammer price.

The general rule of thumb for Auctions would then be:

    i) View the Auction well beforehand and in particular any item(s) which you may consider purchasing, to take account of condition, repairs, construction etc. thus heeding the warning phrase 'Buyer beware'

    ii) Decide your ceiling price for the item and don't get caught up in the flow so that you overspend.

    iii) Note the 'Buyers Premium' i.e. the percentage charge detailed in the Catalogue Rules payable on top of the hammer price.

The attraction of the Auction is the possibility of acquiring a desired item at a below market average price. This may occur because there is insufficient interest at the auction from buyers with an interest or alternatively, the item may be more undervalued in one area of the country in relation to another. Suffice to say that nowadays most Auction Rooms publish online catalogues and any fine antiques or collectors' items will most likely be spotted and bids may even be made online or by telephone worldwide. But it is still the 'luck of the draw' and hence the excitement and anticipation which may be felt at the event. The 'buzz' and anticipation may be experienced just as the Auction is about to begin, especially in the case of a specialist event.

Antique dealers and traders having their own specialist trading areas, will be aware of their own market prices and what they would consider a good price for an item. Some dealers may be more established with better retail outlets or with a customer or other dealer, in the case of a Runner, already envisaged to 'move the item on'. The different trading variations are endless.

It is also, of course, possible to **sell** private items at Auction.

Once again the Seller should be aware of the 'Premium' which would be deducted from the hammer price. It can vary and in some instances, may make it more advantageous to approach a dealer direct.

ANTIQUE FAIRS and Open Air Markets have become well established across the country and will be advertised locally, in dedicated Antique Publications, in the local press or online. The advantage of visiting these is that they are trade fairs and one fair venue will encompass many different stands from dealers throughout the country and in many specialist areas ranging from lower priced items through to Fine Antiques.

ANTIQUE ARCADES AND CENTRES _ These are similar to Antique Fairs in that they offer different individually operated Retail Units where separate dealers pay a rent to display their own particular range of artifacts and a buyer may then often deal directly withe the dealer to negotiate the best price. Unlike Antique Fairs which are most likely held once a month or quarterly throughout the year at different venues, the Centres are permanent Retail outlets or small integral shops in a town where a person may browse at his leisure and the range of antiques is constantly changing.

SHOPS are an extension of the Arcade Centre concept in that one proprietor will now professionally own and operate his own retail outlet with usually increased floor space and full control of the premises. Quite often they house specialist collections and fine antiques. That is not to say, however, that some Antique Centres may also offer a range of fine antiques, dependant on the setup, including levels of security and amenities.

BOOT FAIRS to a certain extent, are proformas of Open Air Antique Markets except that their merchandise also includes general household items together with collectors' items and some antiques fresh to the market. They became very popular from the 1980's, as an extension of jumble sales and table top sales. T hey are a means for any private individual to directly present his unwanted usehold items for sale on a casual basis a nc , clapter in this book, they will also be discussed as a possible good first starter retail outlet.

A first good test, similar to the concept adopted by some of the current popular antiques television programmes, is to allow yourself a conservative budget, of say, just £5, to search among the different stalls and see what you can buy for your money. Some items will probably be priced at a few pence or pounds. Remember to look for items of interest you think you would be able to resell for a profit, including, of course, those items which require some restoration processes, within your own capabilities.

Quite often, a household will have accrued and inherited antique and collectors' items and other bric-a-brac overy many decades and this outlet has the advantage of being able to sell those items without paying auction fees or searching out other sales areas as they attract dealers and collectors as well as the general public.

AN ANTIQUES RUNNER is a person in the business who may or may not front his own retail outlet. He operates by sourcing antiques and collector's items to resell to other known retail outlets and dealers. He uses his extensive knowledge and expertise to comb buyers' sites in search of suitable items to then resell to his contacts.

They are an invaluable aid to established dealers who do not always have time to put in the 'leg work' themselves and this, therefore, forms unique powerful partnerships and networks within the trade. Dealers may also cross-refer prospective customers to trade contacts and other dealers.

ART DECO W. LANGE 'FENCER' -cold-painted bronze c1930

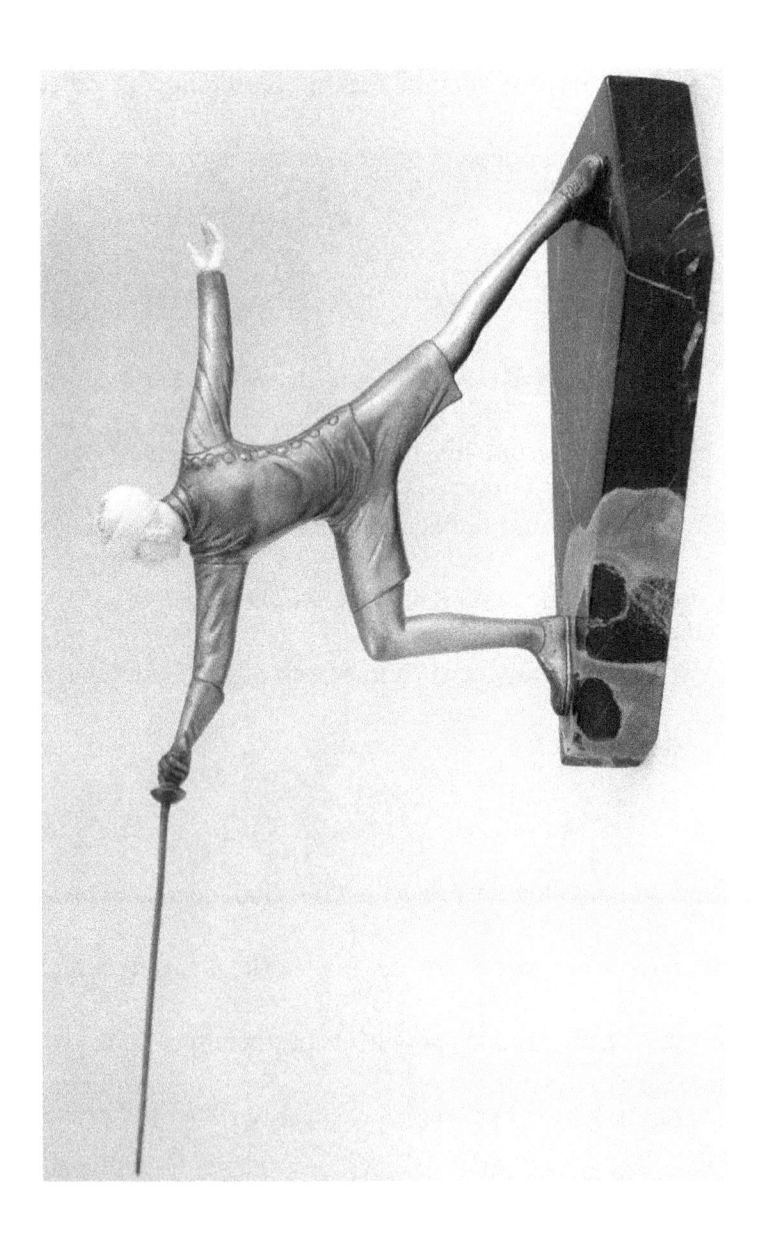

RESTORATION

When restoring an object, for example, a piece of furniture, it is important to research the item thoroughly beforehand, depending on the value of the item. If it is a rustic piece, then a thorough clean with a suitable solvent or just soapy water will initially suffice to remove surface grime. Then a suitable antique wax may be applied dependant on the type of wood.

Other types of furniture may require differing repairs, for example door hinges, door knobs or handles and it would be important to try to match existing screws and other period features. Repair of veneers and inlays are much more skilled and specialist.

If the item has significant value, then it may be better to approach a reputable cabinet maker or restorer as a 'bodged' attempt at a repair could in fact devalue or completely destroy the item's value.

Some antiques may be sold 'as found' which is when a buyer purchases the object in its identified unrestored or, in the case of porcelain and pottery, damaged or cracked condition. He may then undertake to have the item restored himself or to accept the identified 'flaw'.

In cases of unique rarity, and in such an instance, making it the only way to own an item, the inherent damage and condition will not inhibit its value and salability. In fact, it would be preferable that the item is unrestored.

In other instances, where it is evident the item has been repaired, a dealer should make reference to that fact in a written description as in the case of items of significant value, it can quite dramatically affect the price. There are some extremely gifted and skilled glass and porcelain/pottery repairers who may have already been employed to restore an item to such a high standard that it will be impossible to detect with the naked eye. An experienced dealer will have conducted a 'blue or black light' and other industry tests to decipher originality which he will then disclose to a prospective buyer. Failure to disclose such facts, may be construed as deception.

Once again, research and professional advice are the key to good practice in handling valuable heritage artifacts.

Silver, brass and copper require the correct industrial cleaners and it is important not to overclean as this may reduce an item's value or damage it entirely in the case of silver plate. In some cases, the plating may already have been removed to such a degree that it has destroyed intrinsic value and beauty, thereby leaving the item virtually worthless.

Silver plating has been carried out for hundreds of years quite often with copper as the conductive base metal. The silver in leaf form, would be rolled over the copper by hand which is a complex skilled procedure. Significantly, when the plating wears off and the copper beneath is exposed, it is referred to in the business as 'bleed'. Such items, if professionally replated, should have the same roll-over silver leaf process applied but the temptation may be, due to its expense, to electroplate or dip the item. This is a more modern technique first adopted commercially in the 1850's by Elkingtons. Patents for commercial electroplating of nickel, brass, tin and zinc meant largescale electroplating baths and equipment could be utilised to plate numerous larger objects. Also in the late 19th century, the advent and development of electric generators with higher currents also helped the process. Items thus plated carry the 'EPNS stamp for 'Electroplated Nickel Silver' or 'EPBM' less commonly for 'Electroplated Britannia Metal' object. In the case of electric lamps, these should be professionally rewired and earthed. Care should be taken to ensure that pugs are removed from electrical items or, alternatively, that they have been readapted to meet current British Standards.

Some industry professionals may enter the Antiques industry in a support role, initially, offering invaluable services as a hobby, which may later lead on to a professional business.

A top antiques dealer will often possess a wide range of professional skills and qualifications including woodwork, engineering and electronics. Computer skills, marketing and retail experience may also be extremely beneficial.

RETAILING

Having conducted your research, now its time to get started and test your retail capabilities.

Good starting places are car boot fairs.

As already mentioned, boot fairs provide an excellent unpressurised first opportunity for any private person to take part, either as a buyer or seller, in one of the many different regular outlets held throughout the country.

In the same way that items can be purchased for a few pence or pounds, for a nominal cost, a seller may set up his or her table to display wares which may be direct household items, bric-a-brac and some newly acquired antiques. He or she is then in the vicinity to both buy and sell and negotiate 'deals'.

You will experience the thrill of meeting and engaging with the public and be able to gauge how well, and which of your chosen objects sell best. From here you will start to gain experience and test whether or not you think you are cut out for the industry.

Once you have acquired some experience, together with a suitable collection of antiques, memorabilia or collectibles, you may feel confident enough to progress to hiring a 'stand' at a local antiques fair or open air market and the objective here will be to cover your daily rental outlay and travel costs as well as returning an overall profit.

The process of buying and selling is repeated as you reinvest profits back to acquire and expand your stock and ultimately, you will have a sufficient collection to consider renting a retail unit in an Antiques Centre or other establishment. Suffice to say, once you do take this step, you will need to be aware of notice periods and regulations being imposed by the owner(s) of such premises as some form of binding business contract will be operational.Remember too, that as you are committing to paying rents, you will need to make a profit, and in turn, repeat the circle of sourcing and replenishing your stock. At this point, only time will tell whether you are cut our for the job!

You will have entered the retail business where Fair Trading Rules and Regulations will apply as well as statutory Tax obligations.

STATUTORY RULES AND CRITERIA

An Antiques Business is in essence a Retail Business and follows the same rules and regulations which are:

The business must be registered for tax purposes and books kept recording purchases, sales and profits. Even if after the first year, no profit has been made, and taking into account, a personal allowance, and other allowable expenses such as travel and rents, a loss is recorded, that loss is accountable for tax purposes and can then be offset against successive years.

However, as the business proves successful, and if the profits exceed the current stated VAT threshold allowance pro rata for any 3 consecutive months,(currently in the region of £75,000 annual turnover), VAT at the stipulated rate (currently 20 per cent of the full items value), must also be paid on top of standard income tax. Within the antiques industry, VAT is not added separately on top of the agreed retail price as in the case of new items or services, but is paid entirely out of profits. The Industry is not separately regulated and each individual business is accountable for their own professional conduct. Trading Standards and Fair Trading rules apply in the same way as any High Street Retail business and they, therefore, should be referenced and observed.

As already stated, in order to build a professional business, longevity will only be established by values of trust and satisfaction being sustained by the owner in his hard work and execution of the business.

ART DECO 'SEAL' LAMP c1930

ONLINE AUCTION WEBSITES

Online Auction Websites, such as Ebay, are one of the most recent additions to the Antique Dealer's options for buying and selling.

An individual account is set up and for a nominal listing fee, items ranging from a few pence to thousands of pounds may be advertised for sale or purchased on line. A percentage fee (usually around 10 percent of the item's value) is only applied if a sale is secured.

There are options to 'Buy It Now' which effectively is the seller's preferred retail price or 'Buy It Now Or Make An Offer' which is self-explanatory. If none of these preset options are deployed, the item continues to auction within a designated time-frame starting at an agreed price which may be as low as a few pence or pounds.

The main advantage of using this type of system is that there is quite often Worldwide coverage.

There are no monthly stall rentals or overheads and transactions can be conducted from a home base.

Good quality photographs need to be mounted and are important especially in the case of fine antiques where different views of important vantage points will encourage quality sales.

The website provider will exercise control over trade principles. If, for example, a subscriber is reported unreliable or dishonest, his membership is revoked and he will be barred from the website. Also the individual performance ratings, (which effectively are customer's' grading performance awards for past transactional experience), provide a reference for prospective new business.

Costs of postage and packaging are advised by the seller/buyer in the website particulars and negotiated and settled within the terms of sale.

Payments made using Paypal are regulated and secure. One of the main drawbacks of this method, is the fact the item(s) are not viewed in the flesh in the first instance, although often in the case of fine antiques, the seller's descriptions, photographs and ratings are sufficiently professional to assure a buyer and a trusting relationship may be formed over a period of time.

Alternatively, specific details may be discussed by telephone and/or viewing appointments arranged prior to purchase.

In the case of established traders, there are often links to a separate business website supplying information and reassurance of his/her trade credentials and further fruitful business liaisons may be formed.

This trading method can never override a buyer's preference to browse and view a full range of items within a retail premises with the possibility of obtaining first-hand information and discourse with the seller.

RENE LALIQUE 'CAMARGUE' SEPIA VASE c1942

FINE ANTIQUES

Fine Antiques are those items which already have a proven track record and price strategy, i.e. they have over time, accrued a value.

Examples of such items are Lalique, Moorcroft, WMF, Clarice Cliff, Worcester Porcelain, Silver, Militaria, Long Case Clocks, various furniture, Art Deco Lamps, Art, Fine Jewellery and watches and other intrinsic specialist and rare collectors' items.

Their value is depicted mainly by their desirability, rarity, quality and timeless beauty. The fact too, that they cannot be reproduced and they represent a historic period or mood and are in fact, quite often, a tangible piece of history.

Dueling Pistols are an example of such fine antiques. They represent a bizarre period, dating from about 1730 to 1850, specifically 1780 to 1810, when private disputes and matters of honour were settled by dual.

In some American States in the mid-1850's as many as fourteen duels a week were being arranged, although in England, sensibilities against the feuds had grown to such an extent that Queen Victoria ruled it illegal when she came to the thrown in 1837 and it had virtually disappeared by 1850.

European and English Pistols were considered to be the finest, although not the most highly decorated and one of the earliest names was that of John Twigg who was deemed attributable for the introduction of boxed pistols which included all the necessary parts to load the weapons housed in a convenient sized box which could then be carried easily under one arm. Robert Wogdon closely followed in 1785 and after that John Manton. Other makers were also commissioned, such was the demand for personal defence in the early 1800's.

Nowadays a cased set of pistols by any of these makers can

reach £40,000 or more and are highly collected. Many reside in private collections or museums as 'works of astonishing craftsmanship and precision'.

Such was the heightened demand for precision and attention to detail, that it would take gunsmiths about 6 months to make a cased set. This alone could be due to the hammering of the separate already seasoned, worn horse nails or wagon wheel nails collected and used for construction of the barrels necessary for its strength. Also too great detail was paid to the figuring and shaping of the wood and the individual refinements by skilled workmen and apprentices.

They are highly coveted today and remain tangible and awesome evidence of the idiosyncrasies of a bygone age.

Weaponry moved on in the form of bullets which were later used in rifles and guns for the wild west cowboys- colts, revolvers and army and navy standards which are also avidly collected. The array of antique militaria, including complete sets of armour, are a tangible record of this Country's colourful history both in war and peace.

RENE JOULES LALIQUE (6 April 1860 to 5 May 1945) was born in Ay, France and spent his early life learning the methods of design and art he would use in his later life. In 1872, when he was twelve, he attended the College Turgot where he started drawing and sketching. With the death of his father two years later, Lalique began working as an apprentice to goldsmith Louis Aucoc in Paris and attended evening classes at the Ecole des arts decoratifs. He worked there from 1874-1876 and subsequently, spent two years at the Crystal Palace School of Art, Sydenham, London.

At the Sydenham Art College, his skills for graphic design were improved, and his naturalistic approach to art was further developed. When he returned to England, he worked as a freelance artist, designing pieces of jewellery for French jewellers, Cartier, (Boucheron) and others.

In 1885, René Lalique opened his own business and designed and made his own jewellery and other glass pieces.

By 1890, Lalique was recognised as one of France's foremost Art Nouveau jewellery designers; creating innovative pieces for Samuel Bing's new Parish shop, Maison de l'Art Nouveau. He went on to be one of the most famous in his field, his name synonymous with creativity, beauty and quality.

In the 1920s, he became noted for his work in the Art Deco style. He was responsible for the walls of lighted glass and elegant coloured glass columns which filled the dining room and "grand salon" of the SS Normandie and the interior fittings, cross, screens, rereads, and font of St Matthew's Church at Millbrook in Jersey (Lalique's Glass Church). His earlier experiences in Ay were his defining influence in his later work. As a result, many of his jewellery pieces and vases showcase plants, insects, flowers and flowing lines. Lalique Glass has proved to be one of the most coveted and enduring antiques to such an extent that some of his early pieces can command huge prices at auction and for this reason it is highly sought after and collected not only for its beauty but also investment. Some of the original moulds have survived and are being used by the factory in Wingen-sur-Moder to regenerate modern versions. The opalescent techniques, however, are usually absent from such pieces because these were intensive, complicated, technical and artistic procedures whose chemical makeup and artistry was not passed down through the generations.

Lalique's son Mark, who took over the factory in 1945 when he died, employed his own artistic influences and ideas which included the introduction of lead crystal instead of glass. In 1977, upon his death, René's granddaughter, Marie Claude-Lalique (born 1936), who was also a glass maker, introduced some famous frosting techniques. She, herself, died on 14 April 2003 in Fort Myers, Florida.It is important to obtain a full written appraisal and bonefide receipt from an accredited dealer when purchasing fine antiques of this nature in order to be assured of an items's authenticity and originality.

MOORCROFT 'FLORIAN' VASE c1901

WILLIAM MOORCROFT (1872-1945) was born in Burslem, Staffordshire. He studied art at Burslem, then in London and Paris. He experimented with his own pottery designs around 1896 while working for James Macintyre & Co Ltd, the latter being well known for its expert tube-liners and decorators.

He first produced Aurelian Ware which was partly decorated with transfers and partly painted by hand. He developed highly lustred glazes and used oriental shapes and decorations. Some of his techniques were closely guarded trade secrets.

He then developed his famous Florian Ware, in the early 1900's Art Nouveau period with heavy slip and a translucent glaze which produces brilliance of colour. Much of the output was sold through Liberty & Co. in London and Tiffany in New York. William Moorcroft set up his own factory at Cobridge in 1913 with staff from Macintryes. His designs became synonymous with quality design and decoration and in 1928 Queen Mary made him "Potter to the Queen", which was stamped on the pottery. William's son Walter, took over the pottery in 1945 just before his death and the pottery received its second Royal Appointment a year later in 1946.

Moorcroft pottery is still produced today at the Burslem Factory utilising the same original techniques and has an active Collector's Club following.

The pottery in general has achieved fine art recognition with many early designs realising values of three and four figures. The reputation and recognition of quality has remained to this day and there are no direct replicas or fakes although other potters such as Doulton had produced their own versions of Flambes. A Flambe description is applied when the original pot has been refired at an extremely high temperature to achieve red and brown hughes on top of the existing colours, resulting in a totally original colouration. Needless to say, many pots were lost in this process because they shattered under the extreme heat and also as the effects were incalculable and indeterminate, there was no guarantee that the finished result would be artistically acceptable. Those which have deemed artistic acceptance and beauty generally carry a higher price tag and are exquisite.

The design which probably most encompasses the Moorcroft image is the 'Pomegranate' design which predominately has a dark blue background with mellow reds and greens. This design spans approximately 20 years between 1920's and 1940's and for this reason has become synonymous with Moorcroft's dark rich colour tones.

There are many other very rare and collectible designs. Of

course, only a limited quantity have survived the years intact and it is only with retrospect that we are able to compare and chose the most perfect and pleasingly artistic as in common with all other antiques.

WMF GREEN 'LADY HEAD' WINE JUG c1905

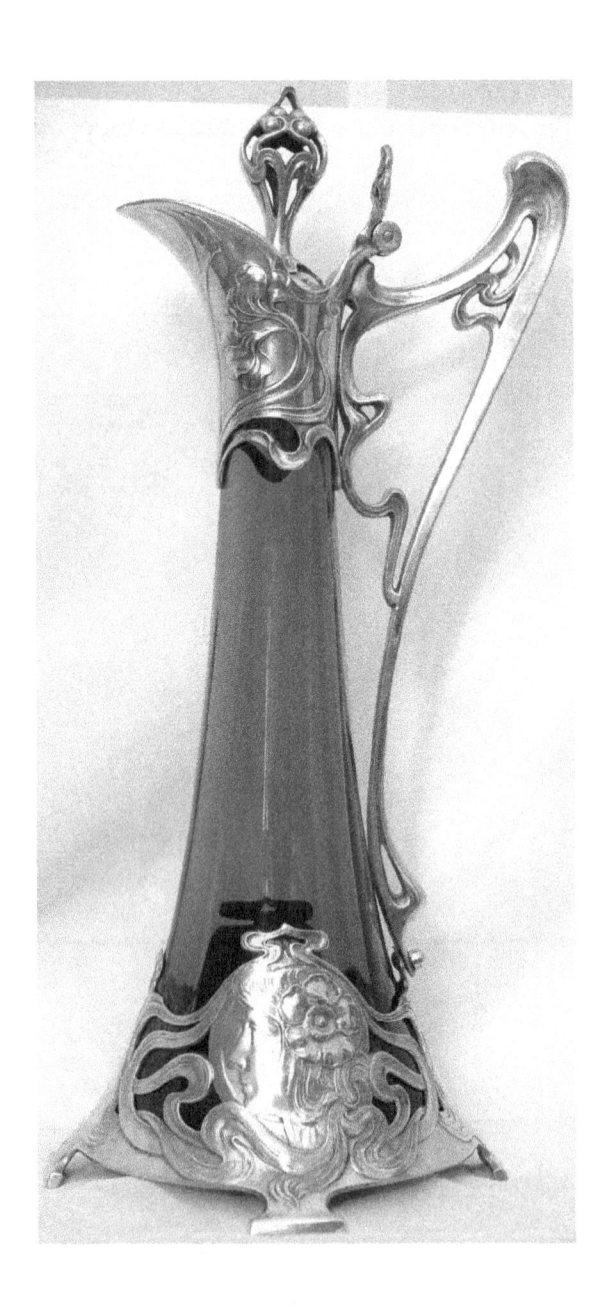

WMF (Wurttembergische Metallwarenfabrik) or translated in English 'Metalware Factory of Wurttemberg' is a tableware manufacturer, founded in 1853 in Geislingen an der Steige, Germany, by the miller Daniel Straub and the brothers Schweizer. It was originally opened as a metal repairing workshop.

Around 1900, they were the world's largest producer and exporter of household metalware, mainly in the Jugendstil, or Art Nouveau style. They are best known for the period of Albert Mayer, sculptor and designer, who was director of the WMF Art Studio from 1884 to 1914.

In 1905 WMF produced a catalogue of silver-plated pewter tableware with stylised lady figures and art nouveau designs and it is this range which has become the most coveted and collected in the Antiques World as synonymous of Art Nouveau. WMF are particularly regarded for their quality and attention to detail when compared with other manufacturers of similar artifacts of the period.

To the left, you can see some of the rare beautiful quality items, currently still available, which have survived, in near pristine condition. Their exquisite detailing and artistry has proved timeless and highly desirable.

It should be pointed out, however, that quality and authenticity is of great importance in the determination of value as an item which has lost its original plating, patina, original glass insert or liner,and may also have suffered other damage, will have decreased so significantly as to be make it almost worthless on the open market.The items should never be overcleaned or polished to damage the silver plating.

JEWELLERY retailing is a huge subject in itself. Experience is required to source quality items, whether genuine antiques, retro or modern vintage styles at the correct price and to develop a niche market.

Once again, to run a successful business, a professional, quality and trusting ethos and reputation will need to be established over several years' trading. This will also include repairing, modifying and sizing (in the case of rings) backup from a properly qualified jeweller and attention to detail. From a buyer's prospective, there are universally acknowledged benchmark standards to help decide value for money:

The Four C's:

* Colour, Carat, Clarity and Cut:
  and when buying a vintage ring
  possibly two more:

* Condition and Character.

On the whole, the richer the colour of the stone the more valuable, but this is very much a matter of personal taste, and the most important factor is how much you like it. Sometimes paler or darker colours can be more appealing.

The carat is the weight or size of the stone which is the main factor in its price, especially in the case of diamonds. The 'rough' would need to be of sufficient gem-stone quality and will dictate the maximum carat size achievable in each individual circumstance. It will then entail a lapidarist's skill to cut the stone in the best way to obtain and display an individual stone's own unique beauty and natural sparkle.

The clarity can vary. Marks within the stone are known as "inclusions" and can detract greatly from the appearance of the ring and, therefore, its value, although some inclusions can add character to a stone.

Some gemstones such as emeralds are known for 'le jardin' inclusions which are intrinsic to is makeup and rubies are rare without at least a few 'fine silks'. In fact, this will often be a jeweller's first inspection under magnification to ascertain whether or not it is a genuine gem. Indeed, in Georgian and Victorian times, many paste and synthetics were cleverly made to replicate natural gemstones as it was very difficult to mine and cut them. Such jewellery was so intrinsically and exquisitely made that very often its value is not detrimentally affected.

Condition is important in vintage jewellery and it is necessary when buying to check claws and signs of ware as to whether some repair is necessary. Character is where vintage rings really come into their own as the same quality of craftsmanship in a modern ring is almost impossible to find and would be outrageously expensive. Rings of this beauty and quality are simply not made any more, except perhaps for the very rich. Generally speaking, vintage rings are generally lower than modern counterparts and offer better value for money.

Once again, it is imperative that correct descriptions are applied to any items for sale together with any known damage or imperfections.

In common with other antiques, there are many factors affecting value as well as the aforementioned criteria, for example fashions and popularity, as well as rarity.

The market price of precious metals such as platinum, gold and silver are relevant, in terms of weight content, measured in grams, in determining an item's value.
Platinum, which literally translated from the Spanish term

platina, means 'little silver'. It is a dense, malleable, ductile, precious gray-white transition metal, and is currently the most expensive natural white metal used for making fine jewellery. This is because only a few hundred tonnes are produced annually due to its scarcity. Its resistance to wear and tarnish, as well as its malleability, made it particularly popular in the early 1900's. Prior to that, silver had been used as it had a lower melting point.

White gold has become increasingly popular. It is an alloy of gold with at least one white metal, normally nickel, manganese or palladium, added. The different properties of each alloy will be deployed depending on the required purpose, i.e. setting gemstones, or the requisite durability of an item.

The karat description will depict the purity of the base gold with an added whitish hue. Such gold is also often rhodium plated to improve the white colour and brightness.

Gold still remains the most malleable natural precious metal. Its market value will fluctuate, marginally, along with diamonds and other precious gemstones.

CONCLUSION

As already mentioned, the Antiques World is extensive and inexhaustible. It would be impossible to describe every subject in detail. There are a plethora of detailed reference books on every conceivable subject available today, quite often on the second-hand market. Also, of course, the web provides vast references on every conceivable subject and is an invaluable aid.

This book is a general introduction to some of the most popular areas which may help anyone wishing to enter this fascinating industry. I hope you have enjoyed reading it.

TOP TEN TIPS

Finally, here are my Top Ten Tips to help start your business.

1. Decide your level of investment

2. Source information on Antiques venues, viz local Boot Fairs, Antique Fairs, Centres and Auctions in specialist Antique Publications, on-line, etc.

3. Plan to travel to different venues to source your items

4. Look beyond dirt and grime

5. Research necessary restoration skills and procedures

6. Research items for history and value

KNOW YOUR SUBJECT:

7. Look for a possible retail outlet and/or test your retail capabilities.

8. Practice negotiating skills.

9. Read lots of books to expand your knowledge

10. Remember, there are always new lessons to be learned. Have an open mind. ENJOY!

blurb